PRAISE FOR
SHE WHO LIES ABOVE

"Utterly unique, *She Who Lies Above* blends and transmutes erudition and invention, image and eros, allusion and alchemy to unveil marvels on every page; to read it is to be ensorcelled."
—Peter Dubé, author of *The Headless Man*

"Knowingly, with invention and grace, and as she conjures the boundless delights of body and mind, Beatriz Hausner tells us the story of the ill-fated scholar, Hypatia, and her student enchantment."
—Rikki Ducornet, author of *The Plotinus*

T0149840

PRAISE FOR
BELOVED REVOLUTIONARY SWEETHEART

"Elegant, thirsty, and visionary poems, echoing with song."
—Tamara Faith Berger, author of *Yara*

"Equal parts intricate tapestry and sweaty duvet, the collection brims with idiosyncratic ecstasy."
—*Canadian Literature*

"In *Beloved Revolutionary Sweetheart*, Beatriz Hausner fingers and tongues a history of eroticism, tracing the transformative power of sexuality."
—Karl Jirgens, author of *The Razor's Edge*

"*Beloved Revolutionary Sweetheart* has a timeless quality to it, slipping between chronologies and myths, simultaneously celestially large and at the scale of a single goosebump. The erotics at its core are epic, musical, sensual, all the while never losing the intimacy of a couple straddling their tandem pains and pleasures."
—Aaron Tucker, author of *Catalogue d'oiseaux*

PRAISE FOR
ENTER THE RACCOON

"This is a book you will wish you could dream. Its cumulative prose lines extend through the essay, the anecdote, the fable, into the realm of fancy, fantasy, and fornicating (transpecies) wish fulfillment. It arrives at poetry and dives through that soft mirror to reveal the ancient machine working the illusion in the kingdom of happiness."
—Gregory Betts

"Bravo to Hausner for a daring collection."
—*HuffPost*

"Not since Marian Engel's *Bear* has the thirst for CanLit bestiality been so righteously quenched. *Enter The Raccoon* brings the reader into a wild world of otherworldly love with arms—and mechanical paws—wide open."
—*This Magazine*

SHE
WHO
LIES
ABOVE

SHE WHO LIES ABOVE

BEATRIZ HAUSNER

BOOK*HUG PRESS
TORONTO 2023

Library and Archives Canada Cataloguing in Publication

Title: She who lies above / Beatriz Hausner.
Names: Hausner, Beatriz, author.
Description: Poems.
Identifiers: Canadiana (print) 20230223133 | Canadiana (ebook) 20230223141
ISBN 9781771668200 (softcover)
ISBN 9781771668217 (EPUB)
ISBN 9781771668224 (PDF)
Subjects: LCGFT: Poetry.
Classification: LCC PS8565.A79 S54 2023 | DDC C811/.6—DC23

The production of this book was made possible through the generous assistance of the Canada Council for the Arts and the Ontario Arts Council. Book*hug Press also acknowledges the support of the Government of Canada through the Canada Book Fund and the Government of Ontario through the Ontario Book Publishing Tax Credit and the Ontario Book Fund.

Book*hug Press acknowledges that the land on which we operate is the traditional territory of many nations, including the Mississaugas of the Credit, the Anishnabeg, the Chippewa, the Haudenosaunee, and the Wendat peoples. We recognize the enduring presence of many diverse First Nations, Inuit, and Métis peoples and are grateful for the opportunity to meet and work on this land.

Book*hug Press

For my father, Joseph Hausner, in memoriam.

And the too much of my speaking:
heaped up round the little
crystal dressed in the style of your silence.
—Paul Celan

CONTENTS

FOREWORD

THE DISCOVERY OF Hypatia's letters to Synesius was cause for celebration among the learned who have long followed the Alexandrian philosopher's life. Despite the tireless research carried out over the ages, first by Byzantine scholars and later by historians during the medieval and early modern periods, nothing penned by Hypatia had hitherto been found. Until its discovery, the assumption was that her works had gone up in flames along with everything else contained in the academy where she taught, their demise, perhaps at the hands of religious fanatics in the fourth century, uncharted.

It wasn't until the poet-librarian Bettina Ungaro wandered into the refectory of one of the former monasteries at Trois-Rivières, Québec, host of a large poetry festival, that the existence of the texts became known. Putting into words the ecstasy her momentous discovery induced prompted Ungaro to begin tracing the mysterious path followed by Hypatia's letters to Synesius to that town on the St. Lawrence River.

Until the recent discovery of these texts, the life of "She Who Lies Above" or "She Who Is on Top," for that is the meaning of the name "Hypatia," was mostly a collage-like construction of details gleaned from Synesius's surviving correspondence to her, as well as historical facts concerning the context of life in Alexandria at the time of her tenure at the Neoplatonic school, where she taught philosophy and mathematics.

The trajectory of Synesius from Cyrenaica is better documented, thanks to his texts surviving through the ages. There are the many letters he wrote to his friends and family, and to the dignitaries he reported to. There are his legendary meditations on dreams, and his essays and speeches. Synesius delved into all manner of topics: "On Imperial Rule,"

"On an Astrolabe," "In Praise of Baldness," and the aforementioned and largest of his surviving works, *On Dreams,* titles that attest to the wide scope of his investigations.

She Who Lies Above is fruit of Bettina Ungaro's years-long labour at transcribing and translating the Alexandrian's words, and then collating her responses to the letters Synesius wrote her. Included in the whole are fragments from Synesius's other writings, which the beloved philosopher likely inspired. Bettina Ungaro presents the texts in as close a logical order as it is possible to discern, with Synesius's and Hypatia's entries clearly indicated. At first glance, it would seem that the work of Synesius sets the tone and the pace of Hypatia's side of the correspondence, though this often becomes moot as Hypatia's discourse tends to overtake Synesius's missives with additional content, including her thoughts on the *museion* at Alexandria, her studies in alchemy (also referred to as "the beautiful technique"), and much more. Thanks to Ungaro's efforts at achieving a final text out of the fragmentary remains of both Hypatia's and Synesius's writings, a deep, almost invisible current is made evident, enjoining the two correspondents. The whole is encased in Ungaro's own divagations. These may take the form of comments around the actual collation work, her own poems inspired by the Byzantine correspondents, or other, sometimes random, poetic flurries, as well as meditations on classification theory, libraries, bibliography, and librarianship.

* * *

I met Bettina Ungaro many years ago somewhere between the PA and PQ sections of the great library. Our conversation mirrored the colour of the books on those shelves. She wondered why the publishers of the Loeb Classical Library series would have chosen bindings and jackets in either green or red, shades that seem to oppose one another, and that I find so difficult to combine when I put my outfits together. "My real concern," I remember saying, "has less to do with colour than with the shapes of those printed objects, which seem to have the ability to morph from rolls to books and back to rolls in a matter of seconds."

The library was and remains the great laboratory, where we go to cocoon and come out as butterflies after days of research.

Bettina always seemed more preoccupied with the manner of making order among things. Shiny silver objects were to be placed vertically, hanging upside down like the bats that often chose to nest on the rafters above the stacks, which served to hide the electrical wiring that fed the lights. We met up often in those days. We talked in obsessive spurts. There were times when we would remain standing without moving, in total silence, face to face, reading each other's feelings. Bettina developed the habit of following me around as I made my way up and down the rows of shelves. I even caught her eye spying through the tiny window of the carrel my lover used as a study space. I suspect she followed me invisibly when I visited him there with the express objective of trying out different positions, using the minimal furnishings as props for our lovemaking. We would often end up with our bodies pressed against the walls of that tiny space. Sex in the library may or may not have been something Ms. Ungaro approved of. At least it was not something we ever discussed.

For reasons related to geography and ever-shifting weather systems, Bettina and I drifted apart. She moved away from my city and began her meanderings in the western regions of the Levant. She had followed a man there though, to her disappointment, her lover proved indifferent to her burning passion. Long periods of frustrating impotence on his part resulted in bothersome headaches for her. Bettina decided to leave him behind and, in order to clear her mind, undertook a trip to Egypt. Along the way, Bettina later told me, she met another man, a former pilot who had discovered the sunken palaces and buildings of Alexandria while doing reconnaissance work from high above in his two-engine plane. She suspected him of being inconstant, yet his photographs of classical Alexandria and the older cities of Canopus and Thonis-Heracleion, as seen under water from the air, were so beguiling, she soon put aside her suspicions and fell under his spell. From then on, I didn't hear from Bettina, except through periodic contact via telepathy. It wasn't until the recent pandemic that Bettina made herself more concretely present.

Her letters began arriving daily in the post. At first, Bettina would describe the strange landscapes she had inhabited during the in-between years of silence. I surmised from her depictions and comments that she was living somewhere in North Africa, though it soon became obvious that she had since made her way back to the small provincial town where she now resides. "You must know, dear friend, how complicated moving from place to place becomes when one has acquired as many shiny objects as I have," was how she finished explaining the reason for her tortuous trip back from the Mediterranean shore, by ship, via the North Atlantic and the Gulf of St. Lawrence to Trois-Rivières, the town along the causeway she now calls home. *Why, after such a glamorous trajectory, would she settle there?* I wondered in one of my letters. "I like it here," is all she said by way responding to my pointed question.

From that moment on her letters became very frequent. There was much to share, yet I worried about Bettina's strange obsessiveness in writing me, causing the distention of those parts of my brain that had become accustomed to the hazy quiet of warm summer afternoons. At first, Bettina's letters were long descriptions of the things she had brought with her, mostly objects she thought she would wear. She described herself lovingly wrapping bangles, bracelets, and necklaces, and packing them into baskets and other containers, which she availed herself of in order to protect her treasures during her journey.

Once she had settled into her northern home and began emptying all those trunks and placing their contents into chests of drawers and wardrobes, the tone of her correspondence changed. Technical discourse took over, as she described the cataloguing process she adopted in order to organize her things. She devised, she told me, special classification systems for each sort of object: scarves were organized horizontally according to type, in ways that more closely resembled the system devised by the early bibliographers of Aristotle, first among the Greeks to build a substantial book collection. (It may be that Aristotle went beyond book collecting and philological pursuit and, in the process, invented purposeful list-making, or *pinakes.*) I responded to Bettina's relation of her discoveries with enthusiasm, emphasizing how similar her method seemed to faceted classification, the horizontal, non-hierarchical system of the egalitarian librarian Ranganathan. I wondered how she could possibly adapt such a method to more solid objects, her jewellery for example. Her answer was quick and firm: "I have arranged those things following the hierarchies invented by the European alchemists." Since I had never heard of such a system, yet was loath to reveal my ignorance, I acknowledged receipt of her answer and shifted to other topics.

These and other idiosyncrasies in Bettina's letters soon revealed her need for deep thinking and detailed research.

Bettina Ungaro is descended from Central European Jews, Hungarian refugees from the Great Horror, to be precise, whose utopian ideas found their origin in the tradition of the Enlightenment. It is in the freedom-seeking spaces carved by the great Rosa Luxemburg, and even Red Emma, that Bettina feels most animated, in spite and against the obvious acquisitiveness that drives her to collect shiny things, like some kind of obsessive magpie.

Her discovery of Hypatia's letters happened by chance one day when, out for a walk along the port lands in Trois-Rivières, Bettina noticed a man sitting on a bench overlooking the open water. He seemed at once familiar and a stranger. She commented on the weather, an admittedly meek way of making a pass. He answered vaguely, pointing to some clouds forming above him, in the hush tone of someone used to living in secret. No sooner had he explained that he felt more comfortable speaking in dead languages than he got up and walked away. Bettina made sure he didn't notice her following him. The tortuous path he chose involved hiding for stretches of time. That day, he hid inside a hollowed tree trunk, much as his mother and the mother of his mother had done, thus establishing a strong family tradition. Bettina would eventually come to know many, though not all, the spaces he utilized in this manner, some physical, others constructed by him in the darker recesses of his mind. The man resumed walking and soon disappeared inside a building on Rue des Ursulines, with Bettina in pursuit. She followed him into the building. No sooner had she crossed the threshold than the man dissolved into the white wall of the main room. In her confusion, Bettina failed to notice the door closing shut behind her. Yet she didn't feel trapped. On the contrary. Once her eyes became accustomed to the crepuscular light of the room, she noticed a series of mismatched chests of drawers lining one of the walls. She went over and pulled one of them open. Empty. She pulled out the rest, one after another. All proved empty, until she came to the last drawer. Mentally praying for a revelation, and feeling something heavy shifting inside the drawer, she pulled its worn edges carefully—it held the box with the writings of Hypatia.

Trembling, immediately aware of the unfolding miracle, Bettina took the box to the large table nearest her, sat down, and thought long and hard on the best way to proceed. There was the fragility of the box proper, and the likely brittleness of the fragments inscribed on the papyrus sheets it held. There was the fact of their being written in Greek. And there was the mystery of their provenance. How could such a precious inheritance have made its way to Trois-Rivières? Obsessive research followed, which Bettina summarized as follows:

> A beguiling man, a predilection for strange furnishings guided me to the drawer containing the box, where lay waiting the disorderly fragments of Hypatia's writings to Synesius. My subsequent research led me to conclude that the treasure had made its way to Trois-Rivières a few years after the building of the seventeenth-century Ursulines convent was completed. Some say that the box containing the battered scrolls with Hypatia's faded handwriting had

been previously housed in the modest library of the girls' school the first Ursulines founded on the Greek island of Naxos. Likely, the Italian nuns brought the precious fragments from their earlier settlement on the island of Tinos, which rises from the same Cyclades waters of the Aegean Sea. Which bears asking: how did the texts arrive on Tinos?

Legend has it that the letters of Hypatia had indeed been preserved by Synesius, who had a box especially made out of alabaster encrusted with jewels, to contain his teacher's loving words. Being the older of the two, it is safe to say that Hypatia, a beautiful woman, learned and eloquent, could not fail to impress a Greek youth like Synesius. He became Hypatia's favourite pupil and, as the writings presented here attest, the object and recipient of Hypatia's love and devotion. Death severed the flow of the correspondence. Whose death came first is subject of some debate. What is clear is that Hypatia's letters went with Synesius to his grave in the cemetery at Cyrene, his 'mother' as he affectionately referred to his native city. How long the box lay with him under earth and sun will never be known.

What is probable, even likely, is that robbers must have assumed the box was of value when they ransacked his grave. Perfectly preserved under the hot sands of modern-day Libya, the box and its contents made their way by ship traffic from Cyrene to Tinos, though likely not directly. The transit of texts and books is mysterious, and the miraculous trajectory of Hypatia's writings to Trois-Rivières is not unlike the destiny of many such records.

It took Bettina several years to decipher and transcribe the Greek original, and then translate the whole of it into English. Her letters to me during that time betray the typical frustrations translators experience, especially when the written object being translated requires suppositions and assumptions that go well beyond linguistic transfer.

Preparing her manuscript for publication, Ms. Ungaro admitted her unsatisfaction with the whole and, in a particularly vulnerable moment, confessed having to agree with her publisher's editorial committee: "These translations often feel like wading through molasses. They've taken all that I have in me, and I've no idea how to make them better. Translating them has rendered me exhausted and spent. A certain boredom with the work and the process that brought me this far has now set in, no doubt one of the perils any honest writer must accept." Alas, I was familiar with the problem. Despite my attempts at helping Bettina with advice I gleaned from conversations with experts in the field, an unusual silence on her part followed that exchange. After months of trying to reach her, I gave up and moved on to other concerns.

* * *

"Credit must be granted where credit is due. It is you, dear Beatriz, I must thank for patiently waiting and not forsaking me and my mental wanderings. You must know by now that I am prone to disappearing," wrote Bettina, by way of explaining the final changes she made to the book at hand. "In the end," she continued, "I accepted my inability to fix my translations of Hypatia's texts and left them as imperfect as they will surely read to discerning and seasoned eyes. The non-native speakers of English among us must surrender to our weaknesses. I am now living under the sign of acceptance." She went on: "Rather than perfecting my work in the target language, what I offer to the reader of *She Who Lies Above* are meditations on Hypatia and Synesius's correspondence, alongside variations, retranslations, and various forms of my own writing. Alchemy is the focus throughout. Being the librarian that I also am, my commentary necessarily delves into aspects that concern the classificationists among us. There is much to be said about making taxonomies function in new ways. As far as the actual collating of Hypatia's letters to Synesius's own is concerned, much of the work was done during a sojourn in Paris, where I went in search of answers."

Bettina concludes her letter with these words: "Here is my persistence, my delving deep into the archive in this unearthing of the spirits of the Alexandrian and her Cyrene, and my homage to their enduring love. When all is said and done, and long after everyone has left the building, and dust gathers in the corners of the rooms, Hypatia will remain The Wise One, she who lies above her gender, its opposite and its parallels, on top of surfaces that grow soft with words as they become warm and later turn cold and solid. Only then can she think for herself and proceed to tell the tale. May the poets and the librarians win the day."

Beatriz Hausner, February 14, 2023

PREFACE

ERE IS HYPATIA's heart. I found it in the long refectory building on Rue des Ursulines at Trois-Rivières. A city not unlike Alexandria, on the shores of flowing waters the colour of sand and summer. Hypatia, she of Synesius, student, lover, and master of the voice of the one who lasts. Hypatia, trained to persist unflinchingly on top, hovering while observing and also underneath, often suppliant while partaking thoughts, receiving pleasure, enduring pain, becoming transformed in the manner of the daughters of Isis and gathering the parts of the world destroyed by those who came before her, only to be broken again by those who will come after. Hypatia exists outside of time's delight and time's suffering, the two knotting themselves in her sex ascending to her womb to be gestated according to schedules made, unmade, and made again by the hands of The Invisible One, who ordered that she be found at this New Alexandria of the mind.

These fragments I present here with and in my own words, in order that their mystery be examined by women and men finally become classifiers, making functional their taxonomies in ways that please and disgust, at once and constantly: The Work is made and unmade and made again by the hands of The Terrible-Worker-Within, who ordered that Hypatia be found by me, and I be found by Hypatia.

Bettina Ungaro

SHE WHO LIES ABOVE

AUGUST MISTRESS

Synesius:
August mistress, Hypatia, called also She-Who-Lies-Above, divine creature, and whatsoever else is honoured in thought or word or deed.

Hypatia:
I welcome your words. So much is contained in these disordered fragments, dear friend, even if they seem obscured at first. I am your devotee, much missed friend, slave to myself in your utterances as the sheets of light flood the room and replicate your luminosity: You lord over me. Come and visit. I have determined to count the days without you, while I wait. May it be that you arrive full-bodied, your extremities and the other parts that constitute your person, in full attendance.

Synesius belongs to Hypatia. Hypatia belongs to Synesius. Their roles curve, reverse, then straighten. Student is teacher, teacher is friend, and friend is lover. Synesius, master of the voice of the one who lasts. This thought came to me while walking along the verdant paths of the Centre Hospitalier Sainte-Anne in Paris several years ago. I went there, guided by a friend who insisted I visit the institution's art gallery.

What struck me, quite apart from the extraordinary art held within the old curved walls of the small exhibition place, was the fact that the streets of that large complex were mostly named after writers, artists, and musicians that I am fond of: Paul Verlaine is the main avenue; the psychiatric emergency ward sits between Charles Baudelaire Park and André Breton Square; there are Robert Schumann, Camille Claudel, and Henri Michaux streets, and more. I explored the complex as thoroughly as I could, walked up and down the geographic markers of that contained city, where my hero Antonin Artaud was first interned.

While having coffee at the cafeteria with residents and staff, a thought occurred to me: *Could the contained neighbourhoods that defined Hypatia's Alexandria resemble the little city inhabited by those whose minds I so admired, and where I found myself at that precise moment?* Being inside those spaces so charged with disturbance and depth shook me, serving as the release I needed to begin collating my translations of Hypatia's texts to Synesius's letters to her.

BEGINS THE CORRESPONDENCE

Synesius:

This letter I dictate for you from the bed of my illness: teacher, mother, sister, daughter, and, before all else, benefactress, the bestower of blessings all.

Hypatia:

You are kind to be writing me in the circumstance. I venture to say that the fevers are your deceit. Mine too. I recall our embrace long ago when last you were in Alexandria. You would speak about your pursuit of the placement of the stars in the dark night, by way of attesting to your method and the manner of your careful measuring of your affection. What I have experienced since is and has been a strange distention of time.

Hypatia makes herself. She is her own creation, irreversibly moulding her person into the object we project onto our own constructions, much like images projected on a screen, that shift, dislodge, then disappear from our collective consciousness.

This all began in Virginia Tentindo's studio in Paris's Montmartre neighbourhood, where I had gone at her invitation. I didn't know at first that her marvellous workspace was the Bateau-Lavoir, so coined by Max Jacob, who often went there to visit his artist friends, including Pablo Picasso. It was inside that space, surrounded by Virginia's astonishing sculptures, that Hypatia appeared to me fully formed and true. Clay, bronze, and gold defined her body and her spirit, and gave me her voice:

Everyday Goddesses

I appear. My forms begin to take shape in
your hands, Virginia, as you give form to

the cat goddess who sits in wait of the rituals
inside my sex. Bastet lives within me, with

and without her antecedents, her hair not golden
but mottled in ways different from this daughter

of Re, Sun-god fierce, who frightens the non-
adherents. I say, approach the woman beneath

these polished surfaces, beauty in clay
skins of polished bronze, gold, even.

Carving deep at first, Virginia labours until
the screams of my muds fill the air.

"Go on cleaving my forms," I say. "In
your hands I come alive with my nostalgias."

* * *

Bastet I become, yes, Bastet and her rabbit,
begetter of the woman in the cat's paw. *Natura*

non facit saltus, softly. Someone is pleasuring
the opening of my sex. It gives onto a temple

where the goddess lives and is delicate.
In your hands, Virginia, I am born of earth

and of fire. After the mold is cast and before
the metal hardens, the molten black substance

turns red to white. Only then will the secrets
of the Rue de Ravignan be revealed:

With you, through your hands, Virginia,
we are shaped into goddesses of transfiguration.

* * *

I ask: Who is Wenet? Once the swallower of myriads,
she persists, ingesting herself furled inside a circle

turning solid the substances that were once unfixed.
Virginia conjures the creature of clay made of

wet mud in the watery abyss of Nun at the primordial
mound where the gods are newly born. I go on

renewing myself as The Goddess Wenet leads
journeys to the Otherworld. She cannot perish.

* * *

Becoming one with my articulations split at waist
by a hinge, my legs turn me backwards-walking

while I am forward-sitting, the better
to become goddess of transmutation.

STRANGE ILLNESS

Synesius:

I am unwell, persistently so, dearest friend, some disequilibrating of the inner ear, where often illnesses seat themselves in me. Bettering tomorrow. But I am just temporising here, to remain longer in your presence's embrace, attenuated form.

Hypatia:

All I can say is, let your little people grow. They will gestate the healing of your humours. And remember this: he [you] is [are] attracted to beauty and the goddess is beautiful, even as the air shuts us off inside itself.

The record points to Synesius having travelled widely in the empire, attending to church business at Constantinople. I assume that he must have known the shores of ancient Greece, stopped at Piraeus and likely saw Athens and its resplendent temples, as yet untouched. Monasteries near Delphi must have drawn his attention. And if he travelled eastward by ship to the capital, he must have seen the temples that dot the Attic shore.

At the time of my visit to Athens, my friend, the author Christina Linardaki said, "Bettina, I must get you to Sounion, where the god Poseidon was once revered." Here is what I saw and felt on that late afternoon:

Sounion

The sea skin glistens.

The columns at Sounion
twist the sun. Ochre pigments
grow into the stone and on the
worn surfaces, the waterscapes
are crossed by dolphins now
between Poseidon's thighs
as he straddles his domains.

That afternoon I heard
voices spread throughout.
The sea god was intoning
the sounds he had held
hidden in his cupped hands

"Ruler of the deep,
 bring forth your octopus,"
I heard someone say.

The artist's hand
shaped the deity,
its stylized tentacles
all around the figure
eight, the seeing eyes
on the walls of the once
room now beckoning.

"Let me remember how we
prayed above the waves,"
said Persephone. (She often
forgot her companions, who
stood with her, mute-deaf.)

The thunderbolt pierced
the waters, cracking
the planks of that vessel.
"He is the undisputed king,"
one of them was heard saying
between breaths, "alone,
always looking for his wife,
Amphitrite, who is prone
to hide inside gales and among
flying fish."
                    It was true:
Poseidon's wife remained
hieratic as she stripped
bare the sea's body, hers.

Such was my record of that
day's visit to Sounion where
the women bathed with the fish
and the temple of Poseidon
rules over southernmost Attica.

PHAROS

Synesius:

I returned from the shores of the great causeway where the island of Pharos commands at Alexandria. Seeking solace from these upturned humours, I went searching for remedy against the downward turn of the letters that flow in and out of my words. There were fiery signs there, and as I made my way down and along the labyrinthine walkways and passages, built on the ruins of what was once the Mouseion, *I lost my way. These meanderings are to blame for my discontinuations.*

Hypatia:

When last I met with my teacher, he described the temple built in the period immediately following Alexander's habitation in what was then but a semblance of our great city: at the main portal of the temple, just above the principal door, was a depiction of Lady Philosophy. Strangely, the disk on her brow featured a cross, which I interpreted as the division of the four elements, and the manifestation of the two metallic principles: Sun and Moon. Before signing off, here is the latest of my songs to the Nile:

For three months
Egypt is a white pearl.
For three months
black musk.
For three months
a green emerald
and for three months
a bar of red gold.

Once a season, Father
Nile, like a lover,
vigorous muscled,
often quiescent beneath
the stars at night, glistens
from above and becomes
dark stone, unbridled
mass of water flowing
into the sea at Alexandria.

ORPHIC IMITATIONS

Synesius:

This is just gratitude for your words to me, August mistress. Especially this morning I am enjoying my reassembly of the bits from our correspondence. In the absence of your divinities, and because I am in need of the metaphoric-therapeutic import of poetry, I send you pieces of hymns I recently composed:

Again light
again dawn
again day
after darkness
roaming night

Again make
supplications
O heart song
of morning
giving light to
dawn stars
in night, dancing
company encircling
universe ether
enveloping expanse
of billowy matter
rising glory
of flame the queenly
rotation of the moon

divides when in its
last phase.

Above the eight
rotations star-borne
worlds, a stream bereft
of stars drives onwards
hidden within its bosom
layers and layers
of matter in contrary
currents circling
about the mind, bending
with wings.

Indivisible division
perceptive perceived
fountainhead and root.

Hypatia:
With infinite gratitude, from me to you, for now I too seek healing from the
downward turn of letters that flow in and out of your words.

THE BEAUTIFUL TECHNIQUE

On a morning like this one, with the wind moving the waters that lapped the threshold of Hypatia's house. They were the same waters I now tread in mine as I pace these rooms and come against the effigies of the Athenian Theseus trapped in his labyrinth, his head in flames. I follow him and quickly understand that a large egg accompanies Theseus wherever he goes. Snakes might hatch around him, given his predilection for other epochs. Especially when Ariadne reigned supreme. "Still, there is a lesson to be learned in the fable of Theseus," someone wrote somewhere, "for his name means light made manifest, and he did liberate himself and Ariadne from the emptied cocoon." So much time is spent releasing light from graves, holding the flame as it flutters in our cupped hands. And there are those who would call this sublimation, lasting years. "Burning waters will be understood as the vital spark that lives at the centre of things," I overheard someone else enjoin.

Such twill-like arguments make it difficult to place Synesius's strange philosophizing. Yet, I would be remiss were I not to confess that the main reason for my seeking out the missing parts of the correspondence between him and Hypatia was to find the echoes of voices that lie deep within me too.

THE HYDROSCOPE

Synesius:

The greatest sorrow was the absence of your divine spirit. I knew, when once I was given to hope, but briefly, that this would always remain to me, to conquer the caprices of fortune, the evil turns of fate. Now, however, your silence has been added to the sum of my sorrows, and I am in such evil state that I need a hydroscope.

Hypatia:

The alchemist Miriam, student of Comarius, Philosopher and High Priest, visited the academy yesterday. She spoke to me of the instrument for measuring the waters you refer to, and asked that I relate this to you:

"At a meeting of like alchemists, I was asked to explain how the elements behave [with one another] when the waters descend. This was my reply: 'When the waters come, they awaken the bodies, and the spirits that are enclosed in them are weak. For again, they suffer oppression, and again they will be shut up in Hades, and in a short while they grow and ascend and put on different glorious colours like flowers in spring, and spring itself rejoices and is glad at the beauty they wear. When you take plants and elements and stones from their places, they appear to be mature, and yet they are not mature.'"

WONDROUS DISSOLUTION

Miriam appears etched in ink before my eyes. She speaks to me daily, this Mistress of The Beautiful Technique. Miriam, first true alchemist of the Western world, known also as Mary the Jewess (*Maria Hebraea* in Latin), and Mary the Prophetess. Miriam, resourceful inventor of many kinds of chemical apparatus. Chief among them is the double boiler (bain-marie in French, *baño maría* in Spanish). This morning I find her hard at work, holding in her trembling hands the winding pipe to distill the *aqua vitae*.

She begins by telling me about four sisters, who, balanced on four globes marked with the signs of the four elements, hold in their hands vessels emblematic of the four stages of The Work. "You do know them, Bettina. They are earthy *nigredo*, or blackening stage, watery *albedo*, or whitening stage, airy *citrinitas*, or yellowing stage, and fiery *rubedo*, or reddening stage. This division of the process into four elements, four colours, or stages is termed by the adepts the "quartering of the philosophy."

"Peaceful is my current state, and it is good," she goes on, with the assuredness of someone familiar with conflicting emotions. "Would you not agree, Bettina, that fermentation takes a long time, and great patience is required?"

"I concur entirely, dear friend. It is a fact that we are required to keep our secret fire burning. Only then can we open matter, sublimate matter, and ultimately purify matter," I answer, tentatively.

"You are a good student, Bettina. As my gift to you, I have prepared a treatise, which I have titled *Wondrous Dissolution*."

Lady Alchemy

Sun and Moon come
together when they bathe
in the waters of origin
at the beginning of things.

The father of things
is the Sun, their mother
is the Moon, the Wind
carries them in its belly.
Their nurse is the Earth.

Mutus Liber

I render red conjunction
before moving on to white
tinctures, emanations
of silver and gold.

Crushing the grains
of Luna I help myself
to words made of
liquid fire in order
to spell your name
on surfaces, letter
by letter I decant
your meanings,
pour my signs
onto the silent book.

Endless conjugations
begin forming at our
sexes.

The purity of youth
has long since passed.

It is time for completion.

Introjection

I assume the stance of
the father eating his son
and assimilate you
and your bright heirs.

I swallow the liquids
close my eyes and see
beyond your promise:

at the threshold of these
reverberations, sulfur
salt and mercury make
your body purer.

Sublimation

Let me know you apart
by force separate you
from your unchanging
motions modify you.

I mean to not err so
you may dissolve me
coagulate me long
wash me and cook me
accept foulness and
draw out of me
the purifying flame.

The Four Degrees of Fire

First fire is slow and mild:
In flesh the nascent embryo
is repeated with divinity
here earthly liquids are poured.

We arrive at the second stage:
The sun in June is gentler
and burns in temperate fire.

Comes the third stage:
Calcining fire strong fuels
the work leading to

the fourth stage:
vehement fusing
uninterrupted supernal
mastery of fire.

Transference

The humming flame is
born inside. Efficiently.
It obliterates fire. It fuses.

Transferring from flask
to flask in my hands,
matter is once, twice,
often thrice gendered.

The consuming flame
is in my mouth.

        Smoke
rises from my lover's
hair, radiance born
of his head, a purer
sun radiates in
each of his eyes.

Materia

Omniscient matter dissolves
remains formless for long
as I place it in a bath of mercury.

The universal solvent fuses
the layers beneath where this
blood pulsates. Unstopping
and before long, transfigured

works and days and
time and sound rising.

I hear a man's voice echoing.
Wrath is in it, as his throat
rends the soundless scream.

Inexhaustible Light

Illuminations follow us:
you are Sol sulphur
I am Luna mercury.

One in the other we are
pulled into obliging
rituals we are forced
to eat flowers made of
luminous glass
and opalescent stone.

Albedo

Awesome you, I say,
as I pull the white rose
out of my sex. A blanket
of petals quivers over you
as if breathing. The air
blanches your lips and
you fall spiraling into
your dream.

Citrinitas

"Supernal mistress supreme,"
you say, as we swim cutting
through the layered water
we hover above a liquid
surface that is covered
with trembling lemons
and other citrus beaten
from the branches of
the howling tree.

The eagle sits on the edge
of the pool, its wings
reversed now facing the sun.

Rubedo

Transfigure my hours
strongest magister
and glowing lion.

I lie above you
my back to your
front your chest
behind me as
I straddle deep
and forward, I,
who am masthead of your
heart, touch and gird.

The circular work spirals
leftward our union with
a more divine mind.

Philosophic Mercury

Member is tongue enveloped
as I draw out the metallic
liquid curve the flow reverse-plunge
the molten matter, so mercury and
sulfur summed together may begin
dissolving, absorbing, creating
your body anew.

Conjuntio

Somatic hands distill, twist
two bodies into one. The liquids
blacken inside the vessel
holding you in binding darkness.

"To better know the world," I
say out loud, as I go deep into
you through me, place my ear
to your chest, listen to your echoing
heart now in the folds
of your legs where love begins.

Often, the reverberations
start orally in mouth where
the thickening vowels slip on to
lips, to tongues, to teeth and shape
sound into closed torsions.

Enduring Ferment

Certain acidities are required
to extract light from total darkness.
In some plague-pandemic spaces
the objects become opaque
and slough liquifies the limbs.

A strange odor infuses the sepulcher.

Comes the golden fire, its flame
brightens the dark and the liquids
begin turning the colour of fish eyes.

I notice a certain frothing, as I
work hard at massacring
various bits of matter.

With you I reach for the transforming
semen. "Fermentation must take a long
time," I hear you intone, "for it is
made by means of our secret fire."

DREAM

Synesius:

In my dream you were all calcination, Mistress Hypatia. Your hair wrapped your seated body as if you were in flames. Someone else's hand was pressing hard at a disk that rested on your chest. On it was etched a salamander. (I remembered, while dreaming, that salamanders live with fire and also nourish fire.) You rose and began to speak in an admonishing tone: "Here is the sign. You must take the proper element now. Appropriate the salt that is central because incombustible and fixed. This salt holds its essence down to the cinders of burnt metals, oh alloy seed."

Your words made strange sense to me, though at first comprehension eluded me. Suddenly, your voice quieted and you disappeared. When I woke up, I found my wrists were bound together, clasped one to the other, as a strange melody filled the room.

Hypatia:

I often feel the desire to be mastered. It is as if I were the master of myself. Hence what follows, which is based on a recent dream:

I had gone to Leptis Magna, in search of answers to a riddle. One day, I wandered into one of the villas that give on to the Alexandrian shore. No sooner had I entered the mysterious precinct than the hoarse voice of an old woman surrounded me. She commanded that I follow her. She proceeded to show me some of the rooms of the place. She seemed exhausted from her own disjointed dictates, which concerned the philosophic stone, and went something like this:

The granules coalesce.
I marry myself
become the stone
lodged in my brain.

Soon the stone
conjugates
with itself.

Before said marriage
can occur the stone must
become pregnant with
itself. Only then can it
give birth to itself.

Like the phoenix born
from ashes the stone becomes
daughter of the Sun
and universal medicine.

Everything is alive.

THE SOUL'S MOTION

Synesius:

My work all the meanwhile, the writing On Dreams, *the goddess ordered it and her blessing she put up over it, and so it has been vowed for her thank-offering. It contains an inquiry into the soul's motion and other related erotic matters, which have not been known before nor yet spoken.*

Hypatia:

Of late, dearest friend, my work has been the practice of transferring the happy liquids in replacement of the bitter ones, to sing the joy as you make your way to your home from darkness to bright light.

Reappraise the writings, dear friend, so that the dreamscapes can be placid, and let me convey these words to you, Synesius. They were left to me long ago by one of my teachers, a descendant of the alchemist Mary:

"When you want to approach this beautiful technique, look at the nature of plants and their origin, look at the air that is at their service and the nourishment that surrounds them, ensure that they are not harmed and do not die. Look at the divine water that moistens them and the air that governs them, for they have been incorporated into one essence."

THE ORACLE

Synesius:

Daily, dearest friend, the spells are cast. The Man-Oracle at Memphis spoke of it when I last visited the place. He explained the relationship that conjoins those parts of the universe that were once separated. As I understand it, it was the one thing he attracted to himself through the agency of another thing. Present in him were pledges, perhaps in the form of voices, substances, figures. The Prophesier stated it in this manner: "When the bowel is in pain, another part suffers also with it, so a pain in the finger settles in the groin, although there be many organs between these parts which feel nothing."

Hypatia:

All I can summon for you on this day is this small thought: Angels are spirit distilled in dream. The heart will always move us out of putrid confusion to light. It is the same light that suffuses my city, Synesius, its streets, the palaces, and places of worship, all the things and spaces that make Alexandria beautiful.

Hypatia becomes one with her articulations. It is her manner of praying to the transmutation goddess, to invoke sulfur-mercury, and begin its flowing through her veins. To darken, to turn dry, other hands must touch her. In this manner gold will be rendered, and the covering of her skin with hard permanence will begin. She will then arch her back, her limbs will soften, and mercury's silvery serpent will finally coil itself around her heart.

THE PHILOSOPHER'S STONE

Hypatia:

Sun and Moon are joined at our source, as I once imparted to you and your colleagues. From the two a single Nature was formed, and it was made living, because of the sacred liquids that flowed there, unendingly, from one to the other and from the other into the one. "In darkness and ferment lies the key that announces the next phase, the attainment of the work," says One. "Alongside walks our purity and its true nature, the philosophic stone," says The Other, as she takes him by the hand and leads him to brightness.

Such are my thoughts to you on this day, dear Synesius.

Synesius:

I wish to reiterate, Mistress Hypatia, that the single most important difference between alchemical love and its replications, is that The Great Work will always give birth to a material child. In other words, The King's Son, gestated as he is in alchemic lovemaking, is the sign of a radical transformation. Unlike its parents, this chemical child is a full participant of the divine.

Overwhelmed by visions, Hypatia moves into herself and begins wandering the landscapes that inhabit her. Some of those spaces are filled with columns and parts of broken buildings. She rests herself and begins to eat the ochre light suffusing the surfaces. There are no people there, only voices that crash against the soft dust coiling itself around her person. She recognizes one of those voices as that of *Mercurius Philosophorum*, god of alchemy, also god of sleep and revelation. She understands that he is to be her guide. She closes her eyes and remembers this teaching from Theon, her father: "A crowned bird wafting its wings will settle into the crown of the king while a double-sexed lion with two tails will perform its dance inside our heart-shaped family emblem."

LIBER

SACRED TRUST

In my dream, I am walking along the darkened cool of the library stacks. *The objects forget that the eye does not reveal all things truthfully,* I think to myself. Suddenly, a large cloud overtakes the space, my ear shuts off, and the sole sound I hear is someone else's voice calling out for the beloved. The man appears without himself; his shadow speaks as if to bring into being his current state of mind: "One eye reveals nothing. The other eye falsifies. When together, both eyes see in ways contrary to the nature of things seen. It is due to the medium through which objects are observed," the man announces. Even though he seems to be temporarily freed from his invisibility, he speaks in whispers, so as not to disturb the fragile equilibrium in his soul. "Objects seem smaller in size when they come to our rescue. It is unlike reading words etched on stones under flowing water," he offers.

There is no immediate comment from anyone else in his proximity.

Feeling the tension growing in me at what is obviously an impasse in the situation, I turn to face the man and say this: "An oar blade once immersed in water, strikes the eye as broken. And the eye, through its own lack of power, produces this effect when bleared things appear to be in confusion." I realize that I've said too much, that an irreversible distance has established itself between the man and myself and that I must now retreat in order to free him from the confusing silence suffusing his inner spaces, which, as far as I am concerned, are replications of another library, not unlike the one we find ourselves in.

As I finish recording my dream, I pick up a letter I received from my friend Beatriz left unopened on my desk until this morning. As I read it, I feel compelled to quote these words from her, since they seem to somehow relate to my dream:

"As you know, I am often transported to the moment when I saw sacredness in the face of my child, Veronica, that littlest goddess of transformation, and recalled these words by Callimachus:

> 'She spoke and with music
> the swans, the gods' own
> minstrels, left Maeonian Pactolus
> and circled seven times
> round Delos and sang over
> the bed of child-birth, the Muses'
> birds most musical of all
> birds that fly.'"

A SINGLE BODY

At Alexandria first was the Museion, or sanctuary of the muses. It contained the library, haven for the sounds, colours, and desires of the world. The librarians were the translators, the copyists, and the scribes, philologists all making permanent the disparate writings and turning old transient literatures, not originally meant for perpetuity, into the eternal. By this I mean to say that before the founding of the Library of Alexandria, knowledge was not deemed preservable in solid and permanent forms, such as books and other written records. In other words, the Alexandrian librarians were the inventors of the archive.

Synesius:
Framing fit words for feeling and idea-making at this end is proving impossible. Allow me to continue telling you about my recent studies. They are centred on the number seven, for seven times did the swans circle around Delos, so that Apollo could be born, and as many times, or more, did the winged eagles engage in combat with the lion, whose strength was equal to theirs combined, but of different complexion. The lion, say the sages, is earthly power, hence fixed, whereas the eagle expresses volatile air. Their long and repeated (seven times in seven years) struggle is harsh, and the lion must be rent by the eagle's beak. Much energy is spent until the eagle loses its wings, and the lion its thrusting. Once mutually defeated, from the two there will be one, a single body, a homogeneous substance some call "living mercury."

These sublimations were once described by Callimachus, like me a Cyrene, but closest to you now, Hypatia, for he was well known to those who laboured in your city's great library.

Hypatia:

Yes, the wondrous Callimachus, and not only because of the elegiac phrasing, which I adopted in that other work I wrote, dear friend. For he does speak of much that is Alexandrian-born, and not just things, but gods and goddesses too. First and foremost, Delos, as you point out, which won the guerdon from the muses, since it was a muse that bathed Apollo, the lord of minstrels, and swaddled him, and was the first to accept him for a god.

THE DISTANCE BETWEEN

Somewhere in the record Synesius wrote, "If birds had had wisdom, they would have compiled an art of divining the future from men, just as we have from them; for we are to them, just as they are to us, alike young and old, very old and very fortunate." By this he meant to open his heart to others, just as he opened Hypatia's. For her it proved as undemanding as opening the windows of her home to the night each time she undertook the measurement of the heavens.

Meanwhile, in faraway Cyrenaica, Synesius seized a hand that was suspended in mid-air, and with it traced the contours of Hypatia's lips so that they took over the entirety of the diurnal sky, even beyond the Libyan desert.

Synesius:
We caught ostriches in the days when it was allowed us such pleasures. You yourself called me the providence of others, and I accounted you as the only good thing yet remaining inviolate. And it was taught us that the person would be consumed in loving another, as if by the art of smith-god Vulcanus, and so completely united with the beloved object that two would be as one, a fiery blade.

Hypatia:
Water, fire, earth, and air come together. I glimpse through my mind's opening a bird trembling in your hands. "Today the beekeeper alone," you say, as your ghost and its replications wake up by my side. May you not set sail to danger-ous lands, Synesius, never venture east of the Levant, for distance will pour itself easily into a vessel made of water and keep us apart.

THE FIRST LIBRARY

Talking echo. Loving prayer. Abatements are drawn by strange hands, mine perhaps.

Following the desires of those that came before me, I go about surveying meanings buried in Hypatia's scripts, the ones I daily decipher, transpose, and translate. Mine is a strange compliance, closer to that of the first librarians at Alexandria. Their minds wished to sing, while they amassed the youthful collections.

Poem of the Library

a

The earliest holdings belonged to and were collected by Aristotle and became the foundation and cornerstone of The First Library. They were mostly all written on papyrus, and were brought to Egypt by Demetrius of Phalerum, first librarian at Alexandria. The books, goes the story, were organized in lists by Theophrastus, one of Aristotle's principal pupils. Yet the greatness of the Library of Alexandria rested on King Ptolemy's vision. He directed all concerned to ensure that his library hold "the books of all the peoples of the world," and thus become The Universal Library. In Luciano Canfora's words, *King Ptolemy gave orders that any books on board ships calling at Alexandria were to be copied: the originals were to be kept, and the copies given to their owners. The collection thus acquired was known as the "ships' collection."*

b

Demetrius worked to realize his King's vision, and under his direction the collections grew "by means of purchase and transcription." The resources allotted to the library were obviously grand, and were directed at the physical acquisition of books, by whatever means, including the getting of content by copying (transcription), translation (linguistic transfer), and original authorship. The first librarians built collections not just by acquiring content through purchase and transcription, they also created content by translating and authoring books.

c

...The Director of the Library was asked by The King, "How many thousand books are there in the library?" To which the good librarian replied, "More than two hundred thousand, O King, and I shall make endeavour in the immediate future to gather together the remainder also, so that the total of five hundred thousand may be reached. I am told that the laws of the Jews are worth transcribing and deserve a place in your library." "What is to prevent you from doing this?" replied The King. "They need to be translated," answered Demetrius, "for in the country of the Jews they use a peculiar alphabet—just as the Egyptians, too, have a special form of letters—and speak a peculiar dialect. They are supposed to use the Syriac tongue, but this is not the case; their language is quite different." Ptolemy, when he understood all the facts of the case, ordered a letter to be written to The Jewish High Priest that his purpose might be accomplished and followed up with a mission sent to Jerusalem in search of capable translators.

So sings Luciano Canfora of the library at Alexandria and The King.

e

Not one person thought to undo the work of those who built and classi-
fied the collections of the Library of Alexandria: nature's terrible furies
took care of its destruction.

f

Quite the opposite is the case of modern libraries,
whose destruction began in earnest
thirty years ago, and continues
unabated, through large-scale discarding,
effacing,
and censoring. To those who perpetuate
the crime, I say, beware,
for the large eye is watching from the wall.
The eye sees.
The eye is witness.

This is how in her writings my friend Beatriz attests to the truth and to our anguish and hope.

PERGAMUM

In one of her more passionate communications to me, Beatriz writes: "Transmutation is revolution, and the library is the obvious illustration of that equivalence. The person who told me this, dear Bettina, was the wiser librarian. He spoke to me in the manner he had of creating a language that was more or less absolute. Yet his words did strike me as accurate, because, as far as I was concerned, what he said was more truly about arriving at that middle space where ghosts persist in loving one another without hindrances."

These ruminations of hers, prompt in me the memory of a piece of knowledge acquired long before my encounter with the man I followed into the building where lay waiting Hypatia's letters, the man guiding this adventure, which my time among the books may have caused me to forget: In Pergamum the texts were copied on to sheets made from the hides of animals. The librarians who transcribed them had become deprived of the papyrus previously and earlier imported from Egypt.

Hypatia:
I have heard it said, dear Synesius, that you have in your travels been associated with the librarians at Pergamum. Perhaps you will tell me whether their great repository resembles our museum here in Alexandria? It matters that you know that several of the librarians who toil there are working, translating books that have until now, languished sealed, gathering dust.

Synesius:
It is so, Mistress Hypatia. I learned much from you. When I visited the library at Pergamum, I was told by the librarians there that in Alexandria innumerable

scrolls, long ago sealed, awaited unveiling and study. I have resolved to visit them when next I am in your city (You will perhaps accompany me?). My intention is to break those seals, one by one. It will be a difficult task to carry out, for the strictest of regimens must be followed. Once the writings are broken open, we will, with perseverance and great patience, decipher the meanings contained in them.

It is said that those who await and persist and find sense in those strange words will triumph, in quiet and without glory.

THE EARTH IS A BOWL

Synesius:
*The earth is a bowl, I write, and I mean
to abide by your pursuits of Egyptian Isis.*

*Perhaps she is that other
goddess, known as Sekhmet, or*

*Lady of the Place at The Beginning
of Time, also known as "Flaming
One," "Finder of Ways,"
"Lady of Strong Love,"
"Awakener," "Giver of Ecstasies,"
"Mother of Images," "Powerful
of Heart," "Devouring One,"
"Lady of the Manifold Adornments,"
and other names too.*

After all, does everything not concern your Isidic searches and wanderings?

*Since all things are related to one another, here is some of what has occupied me
of late, and in order that you may glimpse at my state, I quote from the letter I
sent my brother a day or so ago:*

*"Beneficent gods, why is it that new divinities, destined to be worshipped the
whole world over, always come from the remotest part of the earth? Mercury
from the Nile, the source of which river is unknown, and Liber [Bacchus] from*

the land of the Indians, who are almost privy to the sunrise, and have shown themselves to mankind as gods manifest. It must be that regions next to heaven are more holy than Mediterranean ones, and it is closer for the emperor to be sent by the gods from where the land ends."

Hypatia:
You exist for me as I close my eyes and remember.

There is memory, always forcing the lived life to dissipate before us.

Temporarily, like a slow simmer, the flow of dreaming takes over and we find ourselves in a room filled with wooden statues of litigants, their eyes turned towards the judges whose figures are carved along one wall. An older teacher, likely a colleague from the academy, enters that hallowed space, appearing to me like a shocking vision never to be dismissed: he is standing there, the word "truth" hangs about his neck. His eyes are shut, and scrolls lie piled around him on the floor.

POEM OF SYNESIUS

He is Hypatia's creation.
She invokes him at will.
He is at once above
and beneath her
as she straddles the world.

Remaining loyal
to her meanings, she does lie
above in order to go on writing
his dreams on her skin
often at verge of pain.

She closes her eyes, feels
Synesius hoisting her high above
as the walls inside her
tighten around her image of him.

Hypatia shuts out memory,
allows the lived life
to dissipate, to fade,
so she may be released
to dream another Synesius,
while remaining
mistress of herself.

DEACCESSING THE SOUL

My friend's correspondence sustains me, urges me on to not relent with my poor efforts at making sense of the Alexandrian's writings. Her recent letter deals at length with her troubled time working as a librarian, what she calls her "time among the records." Beatriz begins with:

I was one of the many who once served at the temple of the muses.
We built collections at the time.
We considered printed objects to be living beings.
Extracted from our insides, we memorized the sounds the books made when we shelved them, heard their exhausted sighs.
They spoke to us, and we spoke to them.
We dressed and undressed them.
We facilitated their relations.
We arranged their differences and their similarities.
We distributed their contents in groups.
We arranged their emotions in logical order.

She proceeds with this shocking revelation:

One day, disguised as librarians, the Philistines arrived. Their intentions were not good. Stealthily, methodically, they carried out their nefarious job. Traitors to the profession, servants at the temple of lucre, they were. (Someone claimed to have seen the monsters that lived inside their hearts.)

Their ruination of the library was performed by means of machines which they attached to their limbs, the better to exterminate the beloved objects.

All at once, and everywhere in that sanctum, they set about carrying out their mission: the complete effacement of millions of books. It was usually carried out through ordinances and the setting of arbitrary rules and criteria. "Clear the shelves of all the books not used in the last six years!" one of my superiors commanded. A strange and cold air suffused the place after the enforcers of the villainous regulations were done with their task, leaving me stranded in a foreign land, anxiety's cold needle piercing my eyelids shut.

First, they killed the books. Next, they killed the librarians. Seeing as there were no books, nor people left to treasure them, they killed the library.

Beatriz's words chilled me and reinforced in me the need to frame Hypatia's writings in ways that can express the uniqueness of the Alexandrian's project. How did her reality coincide with ours?

Close reading of her fragmentary record, those of her words that were saved from oblivion, would indicate that Hypatia often found herself in the liminal spaces. Hypatia was and remains for me the mistress of entanglements, for she knew how to lay one surface over another to create depth, even as menacing winds drew the desert into the corners of her rooms, where she piled up her writings distractedly.

Did she feel those strange airs to be prognosticators of darker times to come?

FRAGMENT I

"Is this to be the final season?" Hypatia wrote somewhere. Anxiety must have been gnawing, for long, at her insides, just as Synesius's voice, disembodied, began to fill her head, overwhelming her with his thoughts:

Be kind, skin, become darker
allow lips to remain fixed around
words and let phrasing move
inward of your landscapes.

Open your day, let yourself
become soft feline, step lightly
on this body and recall our languid
afternoons, return us to energized
noisy heat at end of summer before
the cold fell on the stones and
cracked open the desert night.

FRAGMENT II

Hypatia must have risen from where she was writing. She must have moved around the room, must have changed the placement of her furnishings, adjusted her linen dress, her other fabrics, her adornments, before sitting down to write:

Despite the dreaded
suspensions of time
I honour you and
your reverberations
from above. Let
us not lose ourselves.

I work against inconstant
light and begin to distill
your night, turn these
visions into molten liquid
and drink it.

I grow voice stretch
the roots inside my throat
allow the cords to pull
this tongue inward and
outward in sound reach
extend it before constriction
triumphs takes hold
overwhelms the muscle.

THE GODDESS ORDERS IT

The exchange of letters below, prompts me to think back to the story of Isis re-maker of Osiris.

Isis is of the moon that sets, only to rise full at the end of winter. Dismemberment repeats itself in remembering. The replications of dark and light build life. In Hypatia's mind Synesius is made by her, yet together they are re-made with the rhythms of the world. Fire effaces watery untruths, it dissolves them, because untruth is made unclear before and after the waters arrive, flood the land, and then recede.

Synesius:
My work all the meanwhile, the writing on dreams, the goddess ordered it and her blessing she put up over it, and so it has been vowed for her thank-offering. It contains an inquiry into the soul's motion and other related erotic matters, which have not been known before nor yet spoken by anyone else.

Hypatia:
Do you remember, Synesius, the lessons regarding the elasticity of time, when water was measured against flow? Flow was trapped. It happened because of the severed member of the god. The goddess struggled and wandered and screamed her sorrow into the night and persisted, until she found it and attached his dismembered part to the rest of her husband-brother. The waters of the Nile thickened with earth, and the river was restored to the flow of the seasons. The planting of life began and with it the mending of the world.

CLASSIFICATION THEORY

Synesius:
Whether this my experience of ecstasy is not unique, or may happen to others as well, on all this you may one day enlighten me, for after myself you must be the first to have access to this work. But why dilate so?

Hypatia:
Synesius, I have had a measure of what I want, again, and I am not satisfied, again, leading to the main point, which is that you are king. Your whole life should be ecstatic, or the equivalent in joys and pleasure.

Somewhere someone is always representing the things that make the world, substituting them for an object, placing said object in relation to another object.

My ghost comes to the rescue of the librarian who lives in me. "On any given day," my ghost relates, "Callimachus would visit the different departments of the Alexandrian library, noting on sheets the unusual local curiosities reported in the books (trees that grow in the sea, mice that live in springs, and the like). Callimachus is said to have had this thought: 'Depending on the desired purpose, an object is being treated by some mind as if it were that other object.'"

This makes me think of Ranganathan, the greatest of modern classificationists, who, like Hypatia, was a mathematician.

Before Callimachus, other Alexandrian scholars completed the cataloguing of the library of the *museion*, on which his *pinakes*, or bibliographies, were based. Those classification pioneers must have understood knowledge as a multi-dimensional structure, much as Ranganathan did, when he posited that each subject is usually the synthesis of several multiplied connected concepts, that the division of knowledge should be understood based on the study of its facets and sub-facets, or the representation of the same subject from various points of view.

The Foundation of Islands and Cities and Changes of Their Names is the work that interested Callimachus most, since changes in the names of places were often connected with their colonization. Two thousand and two hundred years later, Ranganathan would go on to define and establish:

THE FIVE LAWS OF LIBRARY SCIENCE

1. The books are for use
2. Every reader their book
3. Every book its reader
4. Save time of the reader
5. The library is a growing organism

INSIDE WATER

Synesius:

The work was completed, the whole of it, in a single night, or rather, at the end of the one night, the same which also brought the dream-vision enjoining me to undertake to write it.

Hypatia:

It was the spring solstice when we last lay together at dawn, do you recall, Synesius? You were falling into your dream and I was waking from mine. In my dream I saw myself suspended under water, inside a square container such as they use to hold sea animals, unable to tell whether I was dead or alive. I knew that I would need to come up for air, though also there was the sense that I could be alive, unbreathing, inside water.

It is easier at times to see our couple as one of Ares and Aphrodite. Married by King Poseidon, their melodies were sung by the flying fish of Milos, perhaps carried along by the flotilla of ancient Thera. Nothing is certain, and it may be appropriate at this point to remind ourselves that Hermes was there in the beginning, as Egyptian Thoth, messenger and recorder of the deities, always animating mercury, wrapping the solid liquid around the necks of the bride and the groom, uniting them in a perpetual kiss.

FINAL MEDITATION ON THE MEANING OF LIBRARIES

"Indistinctness obliterates things," said my ghost, quoting her shadow.

Ever the classificationist, I, Bettina, have finally determined to catalogue my dead joys. I am starting my careful placing of them in an order that replicates the relations between species, genus, and other horizontal hierarchies.

"Were these methods especially devised to bring reasoning to the manuscripts in the ancient library?" I ask myself. I have my own ghostly reasons for thinking as much. Some other librarian dispelled the queries and rendered moot all notion of organizing and classifying the word-objects others had so carefully studied, for years.

"At Alexandria," a person once wrote, "the temple could easily be confused with the sacred library. Upon entering the visitor read above its portal THE PLACE OF THE CURE OF THE SOUL. There followed images of all the Egyptian divinities. To each the devout would offer suitable gifts, thereby demonstrating how Osiris and the lesser gods had lived in piety and justice towards men and gods all their lives."

"Someone likely sewed
their tongues one to the other,"
a voice inside me utters timidly.

"I aim not to intervene, nor
imply that certain omens
may be manifest there,"
replies my second voice.

Written indications of things
announce a language like
the needle I use to pierce
the night from side to side.

"We find ourselves inside
darkest time," says my first voice.

"We've arrived at a beach. It is
night, and we are making our way,
cleaving the moist sand with our feet,"
concludes my second voice.

In the distance, further
down the shore, rise two
immense statues. They gain
movement, make noisy sounds:
they are us, representations
of the same subject from
a different point of view.

ENDS THE CORRESPONDENCE

Hypatia:

I say your name, Synesius. I repeat it aloud, and in whispers I utter it like a prayer. I sing it as I do your praises and repeat it again in my dreams.

Synesius:

You have always had such a power, and long may you have it and make of it good use. Even so, the force of your love's spell grows stronger in me with my advancing years. And though there be utter oblivion of the dead in the other world of afterlife, Hypatia, there too shall I remember thee and say your name aloud.

DETERMINATION

So ends and begins the love of Hypatia for Synesius, Hypatia/Synesius who understood, who saw, that without the library there are no books, that the books are the body, that without the body, the book, there is neither thought or soul, that without the soul there is no life. Who knew, in the tradition of the alchemists Miriam and Flamel, which is also the tradition of Euclid and Ovid, of Hypatia and Synesius, that if it comes to be that there is no library of books, there is no knowledge, no transformations, there will be no bodies, nothing will live.

SOURCES

The following are sources used throughout *She Who Lies Above* for purposes of visualization, for inspiration, and for direct quoting:

Blum, Rudolf. *Kallimachos: The Alexandrian Library and the Origins of Bibliography*. Translated by Hans H. Wellisch. Madison: The University of Wisconsin Press, 1991.

Callimachus. *Hymns and Epigrams*. Translated by G. R. Mair. Cambridge, Massachusetts: Harvard University Press, 1955.

Canfora, Luciano. *The Vanished Library: A Wonder of the Ancient World*. Translated by Martin Ryle. Berkeley: University of California Press, 1989.

Dzielska, Maria. *Hypatia of Alexandria*. Translated by F. Lyra. Cambridge, Massachusetts: Harvard University Press, 1955.

Ennabli, Abdelmajid. *Carthage: A Site of Cultural and Natural Interest*. Sousse, Tunisia: Contraste Editions, 2009.

Fabricius, Johannes. *Alchemy: The Medieval Alchemists and Their Royal Art*. Copenhagen: Rosenkilde & Bagger, 1976.

Ferreira, Ana, Benildes Maculan and Madelena Naves. "Ranganathan and the faceted classification theory." *TransInformação* 29(3) (December 2017): 279–29

Flamand, Elie-Charles. *Erotique de l'alchimie*. Paris: Le Courrier du Livre, 1989.

Flamel, Nicolas. *Ecrits alchimiques*. Paris: Les Belles Lettres, 1993.

"The Foundation of the Library: the Letter to Aristeas Version," *The Ancient Library of Alexandria*; accessed February 7, 2023, http://www.alexandrianlibrary.org/?page_id=247

Fulcanelli. *Le Mystère des Cathédrales et l'interprétation ésotérique des symboles hermétiques du grand oeuvre*. Paris: Jean-Jacques Pauvert, 1964.

Gauthier, Raymonde. *Trois-Rivières disparue, ou presque*. Quebec: Fides, 1978.

La Riche, William. *Alexandria: The Sunken City*. London: Weidenfeld and Nicholson, 1996.

Livius; "Synesius," last modified February 5, 2019, https://www.livius.org/sources/content/synesius.

Löwy, Michael. *Rédemption et utopie : Le Judaïsme libertaire en Europe centrale*. Paris: Éditions du Sandre, 2010.

Luck, Georg. *Arcana Mundi Magic and the Occult in the Greek and Roman Worlds: A Collection of Ancient Texts*. Baltimore: The Johns Hopkins University Press, 1985.

MacKendrick, Paul and Herbert M. Howe, eds. *Classics in Translation Volume II: Latin Literature*. Madison: The University of Wisconsin Press, 1966.

Nicol, J. C. *Synesius of Cyrene: His Life and Writings*. Cambridge, UK: E. Johnson, 1887.

Polastron, Lucien X. *Libros en llamas. Historia de la interminable destrucción de bibliotecas*. Translated by Hilda H. García & Lucila Fernández Suárez. Mexico: Fondo de Cultura Económica, 2007.

Samara-Kaufman, Aliki. *The Sea: Of Gods, Heroes and Men in Ancient Greek Art*. Athens: Kapon Editions, 2008.

Yacoub, Mohamed. *Carrés Couleurs Mosaiques Romaines de Tunisie*. Tunis: Nirvana, 2016.

ACKNOWLEDGEMENTS

Hypatia spoke herself into me through years that were markers, often dark-seeming and wearing: the death of my heroic father, as glimmers of his light suffused the horror-memories, his to experience, mine to inherit; the death of my mentor and his twisting cords linking the wonders and the ruptures of the world. Always the light of those who dress the world in sequined brightness: my wondrous daughter and her prestidigitations; her father, and his encouragement; my mother who illuminates the world with the rising and setting suns contained in each of her alchemical eggs; and my other mother, who works her images with light and shadow. From the heart, my gratitude to David R. Carlson, whose gift of the letters of Synesius to Hypatia planted the seed for this book. I am indebted to the poet Jay MillAr, who opened my eyes to a different kind of poetics, and to Albert Moritz, whose expert guidance helped me untie the Gordian Knot in the last phase of writing *She Who Lies Above*. I thank Jay and Hazel Millar of Book*hug Press for believing in the dream of Hypatia from the outset, for their generosity throughout. My thanks are due to Jo Ramsay who copy-edited the book, and to Gareth Lind for the fabulous cover and design. I wish to acknowledge the Canada Council for their support in the form of a grant, which alleviated the financial stresses of writing *She Who Lies Above*. Earlier versions of "Wondrous Dissolution" were published in the annual *Nigredo*, ed. P. McRandle, A. Graubard, V. Oisteanu. New York: Phasm Press, 2022.

PHOTO: CLIVE S. SEWELL

ABOUT THE AUTHOR

Beatriz Hausner was born in Chile and immigrated to Canada with her family when she was a teenager. She has published several poetry books, including *The Wardrobe Mistress* (2004), *Sew Him Up* (2010), *Enter the Raccoon* (2012), and *Beloved Revolutionary Sweetheart* (2020). Her prose and poetry have been published in many chapbooks and included in anthologies, and her books have been published internationally and translated into several languages, including French, Dutch, Greek, and her native Spanish. She is an active participant in the surrealist movement and a respected historian and translator of Latin American surrealism. Hausner, who is trilingual, served three terms as president of the Literary Translators' Association of Canada and was chair of the Public Lending Right Commission. She was also a founding publisher of Quattro Books. Hausner lives in Toronto, where she publishes the *Philosophical Egg*.

COLOPHON

Manufactured as the first edition of
She Who Lies Above
in the fall of 2023 by Book*hug Press

Edited for the press by A. F. Moritz
Copy-edited by Jo Ramsay
Proofread by Laurie Siblock
Design and typesetting by Gareth Lind, Lind Design
Cover: Jacob_09/Shutterstock.com (background), iStock.com/grafoto,
On1 Ultimate Sky Collection, iStock.com/Harvey Tomlinson,
iStock.com/danilovi
Set in Kievit Serif, Uomo, and Xcstasy Sans

Printed in Canada

bookhugpress.ca